May 2, 2006

As Director of the National Counterterrorism Center, I am acutely aware that our terrorist enemies continue to seek ways to exploit the international travel system to plan and carry out attacks against Americans and our allies at home and abroad. Combating terrorist travel globally is a top national security priority. Over the past several years—and especially since 9/11—the US Government, often in partnership with our allies, has made significant progress in thwarting terrorist travel overseas and preventing terrorists from entering the United States. We have developed broader relationships with foreign partners to share terrorist mobility information, designed and deployed sophisticated systems and mechanisms to screen visitors to the United States, and sought ways to strengthen and enhance the security of travel documents, all while continuing to protect the civil liberties of US citizens, with limited impact on global trade.

Pursuant to Section 7201 of the Intelligence Reform and Terrorism Prevention Act of 2004 (IRTPA), I am pleased to submit to Congress this unclassified National Strategy to Combat Terrorist Travel (NSCTT), which seeks to build on successes to incapacitate terrorists and elevate the US Government's efforts to an even higher level of coordination and effectiveness. On February 17, 2006, I submitted to Congress the classified version of the NSCTT, as required by the same provision of the IRTPA.

The NSCTT is built on the premise that constraining terrorist mobility is a critical front in the War on Terror—and that this fight is taking place overseas and at home. The Strategy contains an overview of the many US Government initiatives currently underway to address the terrorist travel problem. In addition, the Strategy describes continuing challenges we face as a nation in restricting terrorist mobility.

To address these challenges, the NSCTT proposes specific actions aimed at strengthening our efforts at home and abroad to constrain terrorist mobility. These actions include preventing terrorists from crossing US and international borders, building the capacity of partner nations, limiting terrorists' access to the resources necessary to travel, and promoting increased information sharing on terrorist travel across the Federal government and with state, local, and tribal law enforcement agencies.

In developing the NSCTT, we considered the full range of instruments of national power. In doing so, we have been mindful that "the end does not justify the means" and have continued to ensure that the proposed actions are conducted in accordance with US laws, especially those relating to privacy and civil liberties protections of US persons.

Combating terrorist travel is a key component in the War on Terror. The NSCTT demonstrates that we are in this fight to win, and signals our aggressive pursuit of terrorists as they attempt to move around the world.

John Scott Redd
Vice Admiral, U.S. Navy (Ret.)
Director, National Counterterrorism Center

NATIONAL STRATEGY
TO COMBAT TERRORIST
TRAVEL

May 2, 2006

NCTC

NATIONAL
COUNTERTERRORISM
CENTER

Table of Contents

Table of Contents

Introduction

Targeting travel is at least as powerful a weapon against terrorists as targeting their money. The United States should combine terrorist travel intelligence, operations, and law enforcement in a strategy to intercept terrorists, find terrorist travel facilitators, and constrain terrorist mobility.

The 9/11 Commission Report
July 22, 2004

Constraining the mobility of terrorists is one of the most effective weapons in the War on Terror. Limiting their movements markedly diminishes terrorists' ability to attack the United States, our interests abroad, or our allies. As both the 9/11 Commission noted in its main report and the 9/11 Commission staff noted in its separate monograph on terrorist travel, constraining the mobility of terrorists should be a key focus of the US Government's counterterrorism initiatives over the coming years. In light of the Commission's findings, Congress required the National Counterterrorism Center (NCTC) to submit this National Strategy To Combat Terrorist Travel (NSCTT) pursuant to Section 7201 of the Intelligence Reform and Terrorism Prevention Act of 2004 (IRTPA).

The 9/11 terrorist attacks highlighted the need to improve the monitoring and control of the domestic and international travel systems as a means to constrain terrorist mobility. Since then, the US Government has made considerable progress toward achieving this objective. The post-9/11 security environment consists of strengthened travel document security, enhanced screening of all visitors to the United States, improved information-sharing relationships with foreign partners, and increased vigilance of the American people and our allies in the War on Terror. Our foreign partners have also made progress in strengthening border security and providing terrorist-related information to the United States in a timely and efficient manner.

The terrorist enemies we face remain determined, patient, and adaptable. While new security measures are making terrorist travel more difficult, terrorists and illicit travel facilitators are continually seeking new ways to exploit perceived weaknesses in travel security:

- Terrorists seek to defeat travel and border systems by using illicit travel networks, including professional human smugglers.

- As legal entry into the United States becomes more difficult, terrorists increasingly may seek ways to exploit what they perceive as weaknesses in US and foreign border control operations.

- Further progress inhibiting terrorist mobility and suppressing the illicit travel industry will require sustained bilateral and multilateral international cooperation, including coordinated law enforcement, intelligence, and diplomatic initiatives.

The goal of the NSCTT is to fight terrorist travel globally. The NSCTT identifies eight key steps necessary to achieve that goal.

1. **Identify** known or suspected terrorists.

2. **Ensure** broad data sharing across the US Government and with partner nations.

3. **Screen** travelers effectively both before reaching and at ports of entry into the United States.

4. **Build** partner capacity to limit and screen for terrorist travel.

5. **Detect and apprehend** terrorists who intend to enter, or who may have entered, the United States.

6. **Dismantle** infrastructures and networks that facilitate terrorist travel.

7. **Strengthen** travel and document security at home and abroad to ensure that terrorists cannot acquire documentation through legal or illicit means.

8. **Collect, analyze and disseminate** all terrorist travel information to key consumers across the counterterrorism and law enforcement communities.

In view of these findings, the NSCTT addresses two main topics. First, the NSCTT captures current US Government capabilities to confront the problem of terrorist travel around the globe. Second, the NSCTT recommends how the US Government should enhance or expand its capabilities to address the problem.

The NSCTT rests on two pillars, each supported by three strategic objectives:

Pillar I: Enhance US and Foreign Partner Capabilities to Constrain Terrorist Mobility Overseas

Strategic Objective 1: Suppress Terrorists' Ability to Cross International Borders

Strategic Objective 2: Help Partner Nations Build Capacity to Limit Terrorist Travel

Strategic Objective 3: Deny Terrorists Access to Resources That Facilitate Travel

Pillar II: Deny Terrorists the Ability to Enter, Exit, and Travel Within the United States

Strategic Objective 1: Inhibit Terrorists from Crossing US Borders

Strategic Objective 2: Enhance US Government Capabilities to Detect and Constrain Terrorist Travel Within the United States

Strategic Objective 3: Strengthen US Identity Verification Systems

Beneath each pillar, the NSCTT describes the initiatives currently in place to support the strategic objectives. Next, the NSCTT identifies ongoing challenges confronting both domestic and international efforts to combat terrorist travel. Finally, the NSCTT sets forth proposed actions, all to be conducted within the constraints of US law and with appropriate privacy protections, to confront these challenges.

NCTC submitted a classified version of the NSCTT to Congress on February 17, 2006. While consistent with the classified strategy, this unclassified version of the NSCTT does not reveal sensitive national security information.

The United States has achieved significant progress since 9/11 in detecting and capturing terrorists as they move around the world. Still, work remains to be done to prevent terrorists from exploiting the international and US travel systems to wage attacks on US and foreign partner interests. By utilizing our own extensive arsenal of tools to fight terrorist travel, and by partnering with other nations to prevent terrorist mobility, the United States and its allies in the War on Terror will continue to cripple terrorists' ability to perpetrate attacks around the world.

Summary of Proposed Actions

Pillar I: Enhance US and Foreign Partner Capabilities to Constrain Terrorist Mobility Overseas

Terrorist Screening and Information Sharing

(1) Develop and share terrorist mobility information with allies to the fullest extent possible consistent with US national security interests.

Capacity Building

(2) Utilize State Department–administered law enforcement and counterterrorism assistance programs to work with other countries to strengthen laws designed to limit terrorist mobility; build political will to implement measures against terrorist travel; train investigators and prosecutors on terrorist travel tradecraft; and monitor results.

(3) Working with Canada, examine the feasibility of developing and implementing compatible procedures and systems to screen individuals traveling between the United States and Canada.

(4) Continue to work with foreign governments to develop identity verification systems aimed at detecting and intercepting high-risk travelers.

(5) Encourage foreign governments to adopt or strengthen current practices for issuing passports and recording incidents of lost and stolen passports, to facilitate effective information exchanges bilaterally and with INTERPOL, and to ensure the effective use of such records in screening travelers at the border while reducing incidents of false positives.

(6) Encourage the UN Security Council's Counterterrorism Committee (CTC) to develop standards to measure UN member states' efforts to implement the obligations imposed by Security Council Resolution 1373 to prevent terrorist travel. The United States, working through mechanisms such as the G8 Counterterrorism Action Group, should work to coordinate assistance with donor countries to build the capacity of states with insufficient resources to meet these obligations.

International Travel Document Security

(7) Encourage foreign governments to adopt or strengthen existing laws criminalizing the counterfeiting, alteration, and misuse of identification and travel documents. In addition, the US Government, in conjunction with partner nations, should coordinate US assistance to foreign governments with limited resources to fight corruption and fraud in their identification and travel document issuance systems.

(8) Encourage other governments to meet or exceed the International Civil Aviation Organization (ICAO) guidelines on minimum security standards for the handling and issuance of machine-readable and other passports. Encourage the UN Counterterrorism Committee to endorse these guidelines as best practices for member states to adopt as part of their efforts to implement their obligations under Security Council Resolution 1373.

Terrorist Travel Facilitation Networks

(9) Designate as supporters of terrorism those who facilitate terrorist travel under Executive Order 13224, and support listings of such individuals and entities who are associated with al-Qa'ida and the Taliban by the United Nations Security Council's 1267 Sanctions Committee to deter others from providing this type of facilitation.

(10) Coordinate Interagency efforts to encourage foreign jurisdictions to impose criminal, civil, or administrative penalties on individuals who knowingly conceal, transport, or transfer currency with the intent to evade reporting requirements.

(11) Increase efforts to encourage other countries to identify and close down alien smuggling networks and document forgery cells, to criminalize alien smuggling and document forgery in countries where current laws are insufficient, and to build the capacity of countries less able to do so.

(12) Continue to work with multilateral organizations, such as the International Maritime Organization, to strengthen international ship and port security standards to reduce the incidents of alien smuggling, stowaways, and ship jumpers.

Pillar II: Deny Terrorists the Ability to Enter, Exit, and Travel Within the United States

Terrorist Screening and Information Sharing

(13) Consistent with Homeland Security Presidential Directive 11, finalize transition of the US Visitor and Immigrant Status Indicator Technology (US-VISIT) system, including VWP travelers, and consular processing of visa applicants from a two-fingerprint to a ten-fingerprint screening system managed within established databases.

(14) Grant the appropriate security clearances to consular, CBP, and US Citizenship and Immigration Services (USCIS) officers, and establish the required technical infrastructure to support the sharing of classified information on travelers with potential ties to terrorism.

(15) Leverage the Information Sharing Environment to establish minimum system interoperability standards for agencies involved in sharing information on terrorists' identities, and to establish systems' connectivity to state and local law enforcement agencies.

US Border Security

(16) Fully implement the US-VISIT system across the immigration and border management enterprise.

(17) Implement pre-departure Advance Passenger Information System (APIS) to improve the US Government's ability to vet international air and sea passengers against the consolidated terrorist watchlist maintained by the Federal government to identify and interdict potential terrorists before they depart the United States.

(18) Establish international registered traveler programs, on a multilateral basis, with partner nations to increase advance information on a greater number of travelers and allow for increased scrutiny of higher risk travelers attempting entry into the United States.

(19) Fully implement US Government supporting plans for the National Strategy for Maritime Security to defend US coastlines from terrorists seeking entry into the United States by sea.

US Document Security

(20) Fully implement and leverage authorities of the REAL ID Act, and develop regulations for state motor vehicle bureaus and state bureaus of vital statistics.

Immigration Laws and Policies

(21) Expand efforts to control borders, address interior enforcement and attack immigration fraud, including through the Secure Border Initiative (SBI).

Intelligence Capabilities and Training

(22) Ensure that an appropriate number of intelligence analysts in the US Intelligence Community are dedicated to the problem of global terrorist mobility.

(23) Increase the number of actionable leads to Immigration and Customs Enforcement (ICE) and FBI by continuing to develop analytical capabilities surrounding information derived from US-VISIT and other border security systems.

(24) Provide sufficient resources to enable the Human Smuggling and Trafficking Center (HSTC) to fulfill its responsibilities to conduct analysis of clandestine terrorist travel and support the US Government's coordination of efforts to combat terrorist travel, as required in Section 7202 of the IRTPA.

(25) Capitalize on curricula currently employed by CBP, the Federal Law Enforcement Training Center, ICE, and the US Secret Service to develop a comprehensive document fraud prevention curriculum to train federal, state, and local document issuers and reviewers on establishing document fraud prevention and risk management programs, intelligence methods used to identify fraudulent travel documents, and how intelligence analysts can support field operators whose work involves the review of travel documents.

Pillar I: Enhance US and Foreign Partner Capabilities to Constrain Terrorist Mobility Overseas

Three strategic objectives are key to US efforts to combat terrorist mobility outside the United States:

1. Suppress Terrorists' Ability to Cross International Borders

2. Help Partner Nations Build Capacity to Limit Terrorist Travel

3. Deny Terrorists Access to Resources That Facilitate Travel

Strategic Objective 1: Suppress Terrorists' Ability to Cross International Borders

Significance

Terrorists are intent on harming Americans and American and allied interests throughout the world. Constraining terrorists' ability to move freely across borders overseas is critical to diminishing their potential to perpetrate acts of terrorism. The US Government, often acting in concert with partner nations, has a number of tools at its disposal to prevent terrorists from exploiting the international travel system. These tools fall into two categories. The first is the collection and analysis of information on matters related to global terrorist mobility. The second is terrorist screening and information sharing with foreign partners.

Critical Mission Areas

- Intelligence Collection, Analysis, Production, and Dissemination
  — Harness the US Government's intelligence capabilities to track terrorist mobility globally
  — Ensure that US military forces stationed around the world contribute and have access to terrorist mobility information
- Terrorist Screening and Information Sharing with Foreign Partners
  — Share known or suspected terrorist identities with foreign partners
  — Detect terrorists at international borders

Current Initiatives

Intelligence Collection, Analysis, Production, and Dissemination

Foreign Terrorist Tracking Task Force

In Homeland Security Presidential Directive 2 (HSPD-2), the President directed the Department of Justice to establish the Foreign Terrorist Tracking Task Force (FTTTF) to ensure that federal agencies coordinate programs to: (1) deny entry into the United States of aliens associated with, suspected of being engaged in, or supporting terrorist activity; and (2) locate, detain, prosecute, or deport terrorist-related aliens in the United States. The FTTTF engages in efforts to identify foreign terrorists and their supporters who have entered or seek to enter the United States and US territories; and to detect such factors as violations of criminal or immigration law which would permit exclusion, detention, or deportation of such individuals.

Joint Intelligence Task Force—Combating Terrorism

The Defense Intelligence Agency's Joint Intelligence Task Force—Combating Terrorism (JITF-CT) provides analytic support to US military and defense collection operations to disrupt terrorist travel and acquire related data. JITF-CT also reviews DOD unique and unserialized datasets to identify and nominate watchlist candidates.

National Counterterrorism Center

The 9/11 Commission recommended the establishment of a National Counterterrorism Center (NCTC), built on the foundation of the Terrorist Threat Integration Center (TTIC), to be a center for joint strategic operational planning and intelligence, staffed by personnel from across the US Government. NCTC is charged with ensuring that agencies, as appropriate, have access to and receive all-source intelligence necessary to execute their counterterrorism plans and perform independent, alternative analysis.

Human Smuggling and Trafficking Center

Section 7202 of the Intelligence Reform and Terrorism Prevention Act (IRTPA) established the Human Smuggling and Trafficking Center (HSTC) as an Interagency intelligence/law enforcement/diplomacy fusion center and information clearinghouse composed of representatives from the Departments of State, Justice, and Homeland Security and the Intelligence Community. The HSTC fosters greater integration and overall effectiveness in US Government efforts to combat migrant smuggling, trafficking in persons, and clandestine terrorist travel. It facilitates the broad dissemination of intelligence and drafts strategic assessments on smuggling and trafficking-related matters. The HSTC is charged with strengthening partnerships with foreign governments and international organizations to combat human smuggling and trafficking. The IRTPA also requires HSTC to support NCTC's counterterrorism efforts.

Terrorist Screening and Information Sharing with Foreign Partners

Terrorist Interdiction Program

The Terrorist Interdiction Program (TIP) enhances border security capabilities of those countries at risk for terrorist activity. TIP provides participating countries with a computerized watchlisting system to help constrain terrorist mobility globally.

G8 Secure and Facilitated International Travel Initiative

The Secure and Facilitated International Travel Initiative (SAFTI) includes a focus on international information exchange. Under this initiative, G8 members are committed to: (1) develop mechanisms for real-time data exchange to validate travel documents, watchlist information, and advance passenger information; (2) provide effective and timely information exchange on the terrorist watchlist and lookout data of participating countries on a bilateral basis; (3) provide input to the INTERPOL database that allows for real-time information sharing on lost and stolen international travel documents; and (4) share best practices on effective cooperation between intelligence and law enforcement officials. SAFTI also calls on members to strengthen standardized practices for secure passport issuance and improve capacities and collaboration to ensure that civil aviation systems are secure from terrorist attacks.

Watchlisting

The President issued HSPD-6 on September 6, 2003, to further the integration and widen the use of terrorist screening information. Pursuant to HSPD-6, the Attorney General established the Terrorist Screening Center (TSC) to consolidate US Government terrorist screening information. In addition, HSPD-6 directs federal agencies to provide appropriate terrorist information to the TTIC, now NCTC, which in turn provides the TSC access to all appropriate terrorist information or intelligence. HSPD-6 also requires federal agencies to conduct their own terrorist screening at all appropriate opportunities using TSC information; and requires that DHS develop guidelines on the use of this information in state, local, territorial, and tribal screening processes as well as private sector screening processes with a substantial bearing on Homeland security. Finally, HSPD-6 requires the Secretary of State to develop a means for enhancing cooperation with foreign governments, beginning with the 27 Visa Waiver Program (VWP) countries, to establish appropriate access to terrorist screening information of participating governments.

Technical Support Working Group

The Technical Support Working Group (TSWG)—co-chaired by DOD and State—is the national forum to identify, prioritize, and coordinate US Government Interagency and international research and development requirements to combat terrorism. The Department of Energy (DOE), DHS, and FBI also participate in this working group. The TSWG focuses on enhancing technologies to detect, locate, identify, track, apprehend, and prosecute terrorists and terrorist travel facilitators, and shares those technologies with international counterterrorism partners as appropriate.

Strategic Objective 2: Help Partner Nations Build Capacity to Limit Terrorist Travel

Significance

The United States partners with foreign governments and with regional and international organizations to detect and deter terrorists' movements around the world. These partnerships are founded on international laws and agreements, as well as on bilateral or multilateral initiatives to combat terrorist travel. Multilateral organizations, particularly the UN, also are platforms for adopting and implementing policies, strategies, and best practices to combat terrorist mobility globally. In addition, such multilateral organizations can monitor the implementation of international obligations, identify capacity gaps, and work with bilateral and multilateral assistance providers to ensure that such gaps are filled.

Critical Mission Areas

- Engagement with Multilateral Organizations
  - Work through the International Civil Aviation Organization (ICAO) to press for stronger international standards on the composition and security features in travel documents
  - Strengthen INTERPOL's monitoring of lost and stolen passports and improve the timeliness of sharing lost and stolen passport information with the United States and partner nations
  - Work with foreign law enforcement organizations to pursue criminal investigations/prosecutions of illicit travel facilitators, including fraudulent document providers, travel agencies, airline employees, and corrupt officials
  - Encourage the UN Counterterrorism Committee and the 1267 Sanctions Committee to devote more attention to monitoring and measuring the implementation of terrorist travel-related aspects of their respective mandates
- International Financial and Technical Assistance
  - Build partner nation capacity to combat terrorist travel
  - Assist partner nations in using their intelligence and law enforcement capabilities to detect terrorist movements across and within their borders, and to disrupt terrorist travel facilitation networks

- Denial of Safe Havens to Terrorists
  — Encourage partner nations to implement binding obligations under UN Security Council resolutions to disrupt terrorist networks and terrorist facilitators operating within their borders
  — Continue to enforce multilateral agreements requiring foreign governments to prevent their countries from becoming terrorist safe havens

Current Initiatives

Engagement with Multilateral Organizations

International Civil Aviation Organization

The United States is an active member of ICAO, which was established by the Convention on International Civil Aviation of 1944 (Chicago Convention) to secure international cooperation and the highest possible degree of uniformity in regulations, standards, procedures, and organization regarding civil aviation matters. ICAO is the sole international body that establishes global standards for travel document content and format. As such, ICAO has established travel document standards that include various security features. The United States, working closely with ICAO and all VWP countries, developed proposed standards for a new system for international travel documents in which identity is verified through the use of electronic passports, or "e-passports."

The United States also assists with drafting new ICAO standards and working with less developed countries to increase their capacity to comply with them. The United States has encouraged ICAO partners to attack persistent and pervasive corruption in the travel systems of many countries around the world and to build foreign governments' capacity to prevent the issuance of fraudulent travel documents.

INTERPOL

The International Criminal Police Organization (INTERPOL) provides resources to assist its 184 member countries with fighting terrorism. In the area of terrorist travel, INTERPOL has established a lost and stolen passport database. Denying terrorists access to lost and stolen passports is an effective way to limit their travel. INTERPOL and the United States intend for this database to be made available in real time for primary screening at ports of entry and consular posts to ensure that, when passport information is received by the US Government, a Customs and Border Protection (CBP) or consular officer can determine if it has been reported lost or stolen. In addition, the US Government is promoting globally acceptable standards for nations reporting to the INTERPOL database to ensure accuracy, completeness, timeliness, and standards for the use of the database in border screening.

International Financial and Technical Assistance

Antiterrorism Assistance Program

The Antiterrorism Assistance Program (ATA), implemented by the State Department's Bureau of Diplomatic Security, provides foreign partners with training on the identification of fraudulent travel documents. This course is administered jointly with the TSA and Immigration and Customs Enforcement (ICE). ATA trains foreign officials in preventing unauthorized access to aircraft. In addition, ATA develops regional law enforcement relationships and mechanisms for sharing information related to terrorist threats and operations.

Counterterrorism Action Group

The G8 established a Counterterrorism Action Group (CTAG) composed of donor countries—that include the G8 members and others—to expand and coordinate training and assistance for countries that have the political will but lack the capacity to combat terror. CTAG provides an active forum for donor countries to coordinate counterterrorism cooperation with, and assistance to, countries in support of the UN Counterterrorism Committee's efforts to oversee implementation of UN Security Council Resolution 1373. This resolution obligates all states to deny safe haven to those who finance, plan, support, or commit terrorist acts. CTAG has coordinated efforts to assist countries to assess and improve airport security and has promoted and assisted with the implementation of travel security and facilitation standards and practices developed by G8's SAFTI. In conjunction with the Asia-Pacific Economic Coordination (APEC), CTAG also has worked to improve APEC countries' port and maritime security.

International Law Enforcement Assistance

The Department of State, in coordination and partnership with nearly 20 US law enforcement and related organizations, leads the US Government's efforts in providing international law enforcement assistance. For example, the Departments of State and Justice have provided numerous delegations to assist in rewriting terrorist laws to meet the post-9/11 threat. Training assistance is also provided by DOD's International Military Education and Training (IMET) program and DOJ's Law Enforcement Academy that train foreign military personnel in improved border security. This assistance may directly combat illegal travel by strengthening port inspections, border and maritime patrol, or passport controls. Additionally, it may impact terrorist travel indirectly by improving law enforcement management and strengthening identification capabilities. Likewise, stabilization efforts in conflict-torn countries may render the climate inhospitable to terrorists.

Furthermore, criminal investigations and prosecutions can be monitored and used as a means for disrupting the activities of illicit travel facilitators abroad. A robust effort involving both US and foreign law enforcement agencies focuses resources on illicit travel facilitators abroad and improves our understanding of the terrorist travel problem.

International Port Security Program

Under the International Port Security program, US Coast Guard–led teams visit 135 US trade partners to assess their implementation of the International Ship and Port Facility Security (ISPS) Code. Additional security measures are imposed by the Coast Guard on vessels arriving from ports failing to comply with the ISPS Code. The Coast Guard also uses this program to engage in bilateral and multilateral security discussions with US trading partners to better align maritime security programs and protocols and to share best practices.

DOD Combatant Commander Theater Security Cooperation

DOD Combatant Commanders engage with foreign militaries within their areas of responsibility in order to encourage and assist partner nations in building military capacity to deter, detect, interdict and, if necessary, defeat terrorist threats.

Denial of Safe Havens to Terrorists

UN Obligations

As mentioned previously, UN Security Council Resolution 1373 obligates all states to deny safe haven to those who finance, plan, support, or commit terrorist acts. In addition, this resolution contains provisions requiring the freezing of terrorists' assets, preventing the movement of terrorists by imposing effective controls on borders, requiring secure travel documents, and instituting measures to prevent counterfeiting, forgery, or fraudulent use of identity papers or travel documents.

Strategic Objective 3: Deny Terrorists Access to Resources That Facilitate Travel

Significance

Denying terrorists the tools that enable them to travel internationally significantly impedes their mobility and can inhibit their effectiveness. Travel documents can be strengthened with advanced security measures. Such measures make it more difficult for terrorists to forge legitimate documentation. Terrorists also rely on document falsification and terrorist financing networks to support their travel around the world.

Critical Mission Areas

- Implementing Global Standards for Travel Documents
    - Reduce travel document fraud in the international travel system
    - Promote the adoption of technologies that make it difficult to falsify travel documents
- Monitoring and Defeating Terrorist Travel Facilitator Networks
    - Monitor and disrupt financial networks that support terrorist travel
    - Ensure that foreign partners freeze terrorists' financial assets, as required by the United Nations Security Council
    - Work with foreign governments to target cash couriers who funnel funds to terrorists

Current Initiatives

Implementing Global Standards for Travel Documents

ICAO Guidelines

As previously noted, ICAO has provided guidance to its members in improving the security of travel document issuance processes. These guidelines have been adopted by the Organization for Security and Cooperation in Europe (OSCE). ICAO has recommended that all governments issue machine-readable passports no later than 2010.

ICAO also has issued guidelines for governments to prevent the issuance of fraudulent travel documents. These "Guidelines for Dealing with External Passport and Other Travel/Identity Document Fraud" are aimed at building foreign governments' capacity to comply with ICAO standards.

Visa Waiver Program

The Visa Waiver Program (VWP) generally enables citizens of 27 countries to travel to the United States for tourism or business for 90 days or less without obtaining a visa. By eliminating the need for a visa and bypassing the checks that are performed during the visa screening process, the VWP makes traveling to the United States—and US citizens' travel to participating countries—less onerous than the full visa process.

To qualify for VWP designation, a country must meet statutory requirements per Section 217 of the Immigration and Nationality Act. Those requirements include: an average nonimmigrant visa refusal rate of less than 3 percent; low overstay and immigration violation rate by nonimmigrant travelers; production of machine-readable passports; an acceptable plan in place for producing e-passports by October 26, 2006; prompt reporting of lost and stolen passports to the US Government; and an ability to demonstrate strong document and border security, immigration controls, and law enforcement cooperation such that the country's participation in the program would not constitute a threat to US security or law enforcement interests.

Every two years, DHS, in consultation with the Department of State, performs a country-specific review and determines whether to continue the VWP designation of each participating country. The country review process requires that US security, general law enforcement, and immigration interests are not compromised by the country's VWP designation. A report is then submitted to Congress explaining the determination of whether to continue a country's VWP status. VWP countries also must designate an official point of contact to coordinate and share lost and stolen passport information with the United States. This information must be supplied directly to DHS within 10 days of its being recorded. DHS and VWP countries will also work toward more effective sharing of analysis of lost and stolen passport information.

Secure and Facilitated International Travel Initiative

As noted previously, the G8's SAFTI encourages its members to share terrorist-related information. Furthermore, in accordance with the SAFTI commitments on document interoperability through international standards, the Department of State works actively with G8 partners to develop and export best practices that ensure document security while facilitating travel of the great majority of legitimate travelers across international borders. The Department of State also works to strengthen international standardized practices for passport issuance, and encourages their adoption and implementation by all governments. Efforts are also underway to accelerate developments of international issuance security standards for the interoperability of government-issued e-passports.

Monitoring and Defeating Terrorist Travel Facilitator Networks

Disrupting Financial Networks That Facilitate Terrorist Travel

Since 9/11, the US Government has focused many of its resources in a comprehensive and sustained campaign against the sources and conduits of terrorist financing. These efforts intersect with terrorist travel in two ways: (1) the financial networks facilitating terrorist travel, and (2) the financial networks using cash couriers to move money outside of the formal financial system. Some of these efforts address issues broader than terrorist travel, but are worth noting in the context of limiting terrorist mobility. The general focus of the US counterterrorist finance strategy is to detect and prevent the physical movement of illicit funds.

Executive Order 13224

On September 23, 2001, the President issued Executive Order 13224, which provides the means to disrupt terrorist support networks. Under this order, the US Government may block the assets of individuals and entities providing support—financial and otherwise—to designated terrorists and terrorist organizations. This authority has been used on numerous occasions to target individuals actively engaging in terrorist-related activities, including providing false documentation to illegal aliens to facilitate travel.

UN Sanctions Authority

The United Nations has consistently emphasized its commitment to countering terrorism and has affirmed the use of its sanctions provisions against those who facilitate terrorist travel. The adoption of UN Security Council Resolution 1617 in July 2005 reaffirmed existing UN Security Council sanctions programs against al-Qa'ida, Usama bin Laden, the Taliban, and their associates; and reinforced key provisions of previous UN Security Council counterterrorism resolutions. For example, UN member states are required to prevent non-nationals, designated by the UN 1267 Sanctions Committee because of their ties to al-Qa'ida, the Taliban, or Usama bin Laden, from transiting their territories. Members of the UN also are urged to invalidate lost and stolen passports and other travel documents, and to share this information with other UN member states in a timely manner.

Pillar I: Continuing Challenges and Proposed Actions

As a result of US Government and foreign partner initiatives, terrorist mobility has become increasingly difficult in the post-9/11 security environment. However, terrorists continue to adapt to their environment, and the United States and our allies continue to confront new challenges in constraining terrorist travel globally. This section lists four categories of ongoing challenges, followed by corresponding proposed actions necessary to achieve continued success in constraining terrorist travel globally:

- Terrorist Screening and Information Sharing

- Capacity Building

- International Travel Document Security

- Terrorist Travel Facilitation Networks

The proposed actions are to be conducted within the constraints of US laws, especially those aimed at protecting the privacy and civil liberties of US persons.

Terrorist Screening and Information Sharing

The United States continues to work with foreign governments to ensure that terrorist watchlists are accurate and managed effectively, and to establish mechanisms and processes to share terrorist identity information with our key allies in the War on Terror. To this end, the United States should continue to:

(1) Develop and share terrorist mobility information with allies to the fullest extent possible consistent with US national security interests.

Capacity Building

Providing training, funding, and law enforcement assistance, as well as establishing entry/exit procedures with our foreign partners, are critical to combating terrorist travel. The US Government should augment current efforts and:

(2) Utilize State Department–administered law enforcement and counterterrorism assistance programs to work with other countries to strengthen laws designed to limit terrorist mobility; build political will to implement measures against terrorist travel; train investigators and prosecutors on terrorist travel tradecraft; and monitor results.

(3) Working with Canada, examine the feasibility of developing and implementing compatible procedures and systems to screen individuals traveling between the United States and Canada.

(4) Continue to work with foreign governments to develop identity verification systems aimed at detecting and intercepting high-risk travelers.

(5) Encourage foreign governments to adopt or strengthen current practices for issuing passports and recording incidents of lost and stolen passports, to facilitate effective information exchanges bilaterally and with INTERPOL, and to ensure the effective use of such records in screening travelers at the border while reducing incidents of false positives.

(6) Encourage the UN Security Council's Counterterrorism Committee (CTC) to develop standards to measure UN member states' efforts to implement the obligations imposed by Security Council Resolution 1373 to prevent terrorist travel. The United States, working through mechanisms such as the G8 Counterterrorism Action Group, should work to coordinate assistance with donor countries to build the capacity of states with insufficient resources to meet these obligations.

International Travel Document Security

Because of enhanced international security standards, it is increasingly difficult to counterfeit travel documents. Terrorists, however, are adaptable and resourceful, continually seeking to develop new ways to acquire travel documents. Consequently, the US Government should:

(7) Encourage foreign governments to adopt or strengthen existing laws criminalizing the counterfeiting, alteration, and misuse of identification and travel documents. In addition, the US Government, in conjunction with partner nations, should coordinate US assistance to foreign governments with limited resources to fight corruption and fraud in their identification and travel document issuance systems.

(8) Encourage other governments to adopt the International Civil Aviation Organization (ICAO) guidelines on minimum security standards for the handling and issuance of machine-readable and other passports. Encourage the UN Counterterrorism Committee to endorse these guidelines as best practices for member states to adopt as part of their efforts to implement their obligations under Security Council Resolution 1373.

Terrorist Travel Facilitation Networks

Eliminating terrorist travel facilitation networks is critical to preventing the movement of terrorists around the world. To help identify and thwart these networks, the US Government should continue to:

(9) Designate as supporters of terrorism those who facilitate terrorist travel under Executive Order 13224, and support listings of such individuals and entities who are associated with al-Qa'ida and the Taliban by the United Nations Security Council's 1267 Sanctions Committee to deter others from providing this type of facilitation.

(10) Coordinate Interagency efforts to encourage foreign jurisdictions to impose criminal, civil, or administrative penalties on individuals who knowingly conceal, transport, or transfer currency with the intent to evade reporting requirements.

(11) Increase efforts to encourage other countries to identify and close down alien smuggling networks and document forgery cells, to criminalize alien smuggling and document forgery in countries where current laws are insufficient, and to build the capacity of countries less able to do so.

(12) Continue to work with multilateral organizations, such as the International Maritime Organization, to strengthen international ship and port security standards to reduce the incidents of alien smuggling, stowaways, and ship jumpers.

Pillar II: Deny Terrorists the Ability to Enter, Exit, and Travel Within the United States

Three strategic objectives are key to denying terrorists the ability to enter, exit, and travel within the United States:

1. Inhibit Terrorists From Crossing US Borders

2. Enhance US Government Capabilities to Detect and Constrain Terrorist Travel Within the United States

3. Strengthen US Identity Verification Systems

Strategic Objective 1: Inhibit Terrorists From Crossing US Borders

Significance

Preventing terrorists from entering and traveling within the United States is fundamental to thwarting their ability to perform surveillance on targets, to conduct planning, and to launch attacks against the United States. US border control measures begin overseas with visa applicants in non-visa waiver countries and with travelers subject to pre-inspection at foreign airports. These measures continue at and between ports of entry and involve all modes of transportation. Interdicting terrorists before they are able to set foot on American soil limits the serious problem of locating terrorists who have gained access to the United States. If terrorists have made their way into the United States, capturing them as they travel within the country is of paramount national security concern. Moreover, the United States must be prepared to capture terrorists who—after planning or conducting operational activities—attempt to leave the country.

Critical Mission Areas

- Visa Screening Process
- Western Hemisphere Partnerships
  - Strengthen North American borders by requiring US citizens and all foreign nationals to present a passport or other secure document when crossing international borders
  - Prevent terrorists from entering countries in the Western Hemisphere while ensuring streamlined movement of legitimate travelers and cargo
- Domestic Risk Management Initiatives—Traveler Screening and Inspection Processes

- — Share known or suspected terrorist identities with immigration, border, and law enforcement officials across the US Government
- Border Security Initiatives
  - — Prevent terrorists from entering the United States through land, sea, and air ports of entry, and increase enforcement between ports of entry
  - — Detect and prevent terrorists and terrorist weapons from entering the United States
  - — Increase interior enforcement of US immigration laws to locate, detain, and remove terrorists who have entered the United States
  - — Prevent the US maritime industry from being used by terrorists to infiltrate the United States
  - — Enhance maritime surveillance capabilities to achieve an effective understanding of anything associated with the maritime domain that could impact the security, safety, economy, or environment of the United States within US territorial seas and internal waters

Current Initiatives

Visa Screening Process

Visas Viper Program

The Visas Viper Program, instituted in 1993, is a Department of State mechanism used to enter suspected terrorists' names into appropriate watchlists. This ensures that suspected terrorists are identified appropriately should they later apply for visas or entry into the United States. The Viper Program first was intended to disseminate information on potential terrorists to US embassies and consular posts around the world and is now a powerful tool for US Border Patrol authorities.

Visas Condor Program

The Visas Condor Program, instituted in 2002, is a mechanism that requires consular officials to refer certain visa cases to law enforcement and intelligence agencies for further review under the visa Security Advisory Opinion (SAO) process. The SAO process enables consular officers to confirm visa applicants' eligibility to travel to the United States.

Consolidated Consular Database

The Consolidated Consular Database (CCD) maintains detailed information in a single system, including photos of all overseas visa applicants. Data from all visa applicants is relayed for use at ports of entry.

Visa Waiver Program

As discussed previously, 27 countries participate in the US Visa Waiver Program (VWP), which generally allows nationals from those countries to enter and remain in the United States for up to 90 days without a visa for tourism or business purposes. The VWP currently requires that participating countries issue machine-readable passports. This will enable inspectors at the border and ports of entry to validate electronically a traveler's identification and travel documents.

Visa Security Program

Immigration and Customs Enforcement (ICE) has deployed senior special agents to serve as ICE Visa Security Officers (VSOs) in selected US embassies and consulates overseas as part of the Visa Security Program. ICE VSOs have extensive expertise in the full range of border enforcement functions, and training and experience in key subject matter areas such as counterterrorism investigations, document examination, interview techniques, intelligence research, and immigration and national security law.

Western Hemisphere Partnerships

Western Hemisphere Travel Initiative

The Western Hemisphere Travel Initiative (WHTI), announced in 2005, resulted from a mandate within the IRTPA for the Secretaries of Homeland Security and State to develop and implement a plan that requires US citizens and foreign nationals to present a passport or other secure document when entering the United States. The WHTI requires by January 2008 that the US Government have a plan in place for all US citizens, citizens of the British Overseas Territory of Bermuda, and citizens of Canada and Mexico to present a passport or other secure document that establishes the bearer's identity and nationality upon entry or return to the United States.

Security and Prosperity Partnership

The Security and Prosperity Partnership (SPP) establishes a common security strategy for Canada, Mexico, and the United States to prevent terrorists from entering these countries while ensuring streamlined movement of legitimate travelers and cargo across shared North American borders. The goals of SPP are threefold: (1) secure North America from external threats; (2) prevent and respond to threats within North America; and, (3) further streamline the secure movement of low-risk traffic across shared North American borders.

North American Aerospace Defense Command

The North American Aerospace Defense Command (NORAD) conducts aerospace warning and control operations to deter, detect, interdict and, if necessary, defeat air threats to North America, including those posed by terrorists.

Domestic Risk Management Initiatives—Traveler Screening and Inspection Processes

Terrorist Screening Center

The 9/11 attacks prompted significant enhancements in how the US Government screens for potential terrorists attempting to enter the United States and how screening information is shared with law enforcement agencies and transportation carriers. In September 2003, the President signed HSPD-6, which ordered the establishment of the Terrorist Screening Center (TSC) to create a consolidated US Government terrorist watchlist and make it available to relevant US agencies and appropriate private sector entities at home and abroad—from consular officers and Border Patrol agents, to state and local law enforcement, to US airlines. The TSC receives information on terrorist identities from various US Government agencies and departments.

Customs and Border Protection Initiatives

At US borders, CBP exercises its priority mission of preventing terrorists from entering the United States without unduly impeding legitimate travel. CBP's approximately 20,000 law enforcement officers employ a layered, risk-management approach to identify and interdict potential terrorists attempting to enter the United States using sophisticated automated analytical tools, extensive anti-terrorism training, national policy and procedures, close Interagency coordination, and effective international cooperation. In addition, CBP Border Patrol agents perform checks to verify that individuals apprehended while attempting to enter the United States illegally between ports of entry do not have terrorist ties.

At ports of entry, CBP has instituted Counterterrorism Response (CR) protocols that require thorough questioning and searching, as appropriate, of subjects who are suspected of having ties to terrorists. Port of entry personnel determine admissibility and deny entry when a traveler may pose a threat.

National Targeting Center

CBP's National Targeting Center (NTC) conducts national level targeting and analysis in support of border-related efforts to identify and interdict terrorists. Established in November 2001, NTC's primary mission is to provide round-the-clock tactical targeting and analytical support for CBP antiterrorism efforts. In January 2005, CBP created a Fraudulent Document Analysis Unit (FDAU) to support the removal of fraudulent travel documents from circulation. The NTC supports all CBP field elements, as well as ICE and US Citizenship and Immigration Services (USCIS).

US-VISIT

United States Visitor and Immigrant Status Indicator Technology (US-VISIT) encompasses a series of measures that enable DHS and State to conduct watchlist checks and confirm the identities of travelers seeking to enter the United States. US-VISIT is part of a continuum of security measures that begins overseas and continues through a visitor's arrival in and departure from the United States. US-VISIT incorporates eligibility determinations made by both the Departments of Homeland Security and State to facilitate legitimate travel while enhancing the security of US visitors and citizens.

Registered Traveler Program

DHS is working with US and international partners to expand and enhance international registered traveler programs to improve risk management by consolidating travelers' required information.

Advance Passenger Information System

The Advance Passenger Information System (APIS) was developed by the legacy US Customs Service in 1988. Airline carriers collect passenger and crew data from the plane manifest and transmit this data to the CBP Data Center. CBP uses APIS to identify suspect passengers, while facilitating the majority of law-abiding passengers through the clearance process. APIS information can be used to interdict and apprehend potential terrorists before they depart the United States.

US Border Security Initiatives

Secure Border Initiative

The Secure Border Initiative (SBI) is a comprehensive plan to secure America's borders and reduce the threat posed by illegal migration. SBI is composed of five key elements:

- Increase the number of agents patrolling US borders, securing our ports of entry, and enforcing immigration laws

- Expand detention and removal capabilities

- Implement a comprehensive and systemic upgrading of the technology used in controlling the border

- Increase investment in infrastructure improvements at the border—providing additional physical security to sharply reduce illegal border crossings

- Increase interior enforcement of our immigration laws—including more robust worksite enforcement

The SBI focuses broadly on three major areas of enforcement. The first area is border control in order to prevent illegal entry through security breaches. The second area deals with immigration enforcement, such as locating, detaining, and removing aliens who are present in the United States in violation of our laws. The third area addresses immigration reform through legislation.

National Strategy for Maritime Security

In addition to entry into the United States by land and air, terrorists may attempt to travel by sea and enter the country along US coastlines. In September 2005, the US Government published the National Strategy for Maritime Security (NSMS), an integrated set of plans and objectives aimed at: (1) strengthening US capabilities to protect the nation's critical maritime interests; (2) preventing terrorists and rogue states from exploiting the maritime domain to attack US interests; and (3) defending US coastlines from terrorist entry. The strategy, composed of an overarching national strategy and eight supporting component plans, articulates efforts to be undertaken across the Federal government, with state and local law enforcement agencies, and the private sector to guard against maritime threats to national security. The following three component plans are of particular relevance to this NSCTT.

The Maritime Operational Threat Response Plan, one of the supporting plans of the NSMS, establishes requirements for coordination between US Government maritime agencies, coordination protocols, and agency roles and responsibilities to enable the Federal government to respond quickly and decisively to threats. Such threats include but are not limited to terrorists attempting to exploit the maritime domain to conduct attacks against the United States or commit illegal acts, including unlawful entry to the United States.

The National Plan to Achieve Maritime Domain Awareness, which also supports the NSMS, lays the foundation for achieving an effective understanding of anything associated with the maritime domain that could impact the security, safety, economy, or environment of the United States, and aims to identify threats as early and as distant from US shores as possible.

The International Outreach Plan, also developed to support the National Strategy for Maritime Security, directs the Department of State to coordinate all maritime security initiatives undertaken with foreign governments and international organizations, and solicits international support for enhanced maritime security.

COASTWATCH Program

The mission of the COASTWATCH program is to identify vessels of interest that may elicit national security concerns because of suspect people or cargo aboard, suspect business practices, or suspect crew or ownership associations. Conducted in partnership with the Office of Naval Intelligence and CBP, COASTWATCH observes suspected vessels until their arrival at US ports.

Coast Guard Notice of Arrival Screening

A US Coast Guard National Vessel Movement Center (NVMC) has been established to receive vessel advance Notice of Arrival (NOA) reports and screen crew lists against various watchlists.

Strategic Objective 2: Enhance US Government Capabilities to Detect and Constrain Terrorist Travel Within the United States

Significance

The United States faces capable and adaptive enemies who may reside within US borders—legally or illegally—and conduct activities clandestinely. Terrorists seek individuals who have both the expertise and ability to enter and reside in the United States to conduct reconnaissance of the attack area, practice dry runs, and eventually conduct the attack. Terrorists also require logistical support in the United States to facilitate transportation, safe housing, and financial transactions.

In many cases, information on these terrorists can be derived from the vast array of US and foreign investigative and intelligence databases. Interior immigration enforcement mechanisms and better training for screening at federal, state, and local levels will magnify the US Government's ability to detect and constrain terrorists who have entered the United States. Enhancing the US Government's ability to detect and constrain terrorist travel within the United States could result in preventing the next terrorist attack against the Homeland.

Critical Mission Areas

- Coordination and Information Sharing between State and Local Law Enforcement and the Federal Government
  - Share relevant Homeland security and terrorism information among Federal, state, and local government entities to detect and constrain terrorist movement within the United States
  - Identify, investigate, and disrupt terrorist travel-related threats to the United States
- Transportation Security Measures
  - Strengthen US transportation security by screening all passengers, operators, crew members, and baggage
  - Enhance aircraft security by providing air marshals aboard flights traveling to or within the United States

Current Initiatives

Coordination and Information Sharing Between State and Local Law Enforcement and the Federal Government

Intelligence Reform and Terrorism Prevention Act of 2004

The Intelligence Reform and Terrorism Prevention Act of 2004 (IRTPA) created the position of the Director of National Intelligence (DNI), tasked to lead a unified Intelligence Community. The IRTPA, through the Office of the Director of National Intelligence (ODNI), also created the position of Information Sharing Program Manager, who is tasked with overseeing the implementation and management of an Information Sharing Environment (ISE) to facilitate the sharing of terrorism information, including terrorist screening information across the US Government and with foreign partners. The President issued requirements and guidelines for establishing the ISE on December 16, 2005. In addition, the IRTPA establishes mechanisms that improve transportation security, such as airline passenger pre-screening, detection equipment at ports of entry, and employment of federal air marshals.

Homeland Security Act

In November 2002, the President signed into law the Homeland Security Act. Provisions of this law require federal agencies to: (1) share relevant and appropriate Homeland security information with other federal agencies and appropriate state and local personnel; (2) identify and safeguard Homeland security information that is sensitive but unclassified; and (3) determine whether, how, and to what extent to remove classified sources and methods to facilitate information sharing. As with the IRTPA, this legislation fosters the dissemination to appropriate parties of terrorist travel-related data pertaining to potential threats to the United States, US interests, and allies.

Joint Terrorism Task Forces

FBI-led Joint Terrorism Task Forces (JTTFs) were established in the 1980s and grew significantly after 9/11. The JTTFs serve three main purposes: (1) prevent terrorist attacks; (2) respond to and investigate terrorist incidents or terrorist-related activity; and (3) identify and investigate domestic and foreign terrorist groups and individuals targeting or operating within the United States. The cooperation and coordination fostered by the JTTFs between local, state, and federal agencies has resulted in a number of successful operations to thwart terrorist activity inside the United States.

Today, JTTFs exist in 103 cities throughout the nation, with at least one in each of the FBI's 56 field offices, as well as others in outlying FBI resident agency annexes. The National JTTF (N-JTTF), located at FBI headquarters, includes representatives from a number of other agencies. Local JTTFs are composed of participants from federal agencies as well as state and local law enforcement personnel. As the frontline against terrorism, JTTF members are highly trained and locally based, and include investigators, analysts, linguists, SWAT experts, and other specialists.

Immigration and Customs Enforcement Initiatives

Immigration and Customs Enforcement (ICE) has established or realigned a number of organizational entities to assist in identifying, investigating, and disrupting terrorist threats against the Homeland. The ICE National Security and Threat Protection Unit works with various members of the Intelligence Community to identify and develop national level initiatives that support the War on Terror. Similarly, the ICE Compliance Enforcement Unit oversees the generation and assignment of leads about individuals who have overstayed their visas or who have violated the National Security Entry-Exit Registration Program (NSEERS), the Student and Exchange Visitor Information System (SEVIS), or the Visa Revocation program. In addition, the ICE Law Enforcement Support Center (LESC) is a national, single point-of-contact entity that provides timely immigration status and identity information and real-time assistance to the entire local, state and federal Law Enforcement community on immigrants suspected, arrested, or convicted of criminal activity.

The ICE Threat Analysis Section (TAS) is also tasked with identifying individuals previously unknown to authorities who may pose a threat to national security. Additionally, the ICE office of investigations created a liaison section at the CBP's NTC that is staffed by ICE special agents. Anytime CBP is notified of an inbound watchlisted individual, an ICE special agent will respond at the port of entry to conduct an interview of the watchlisted subject.

Executive Order 13388

Signed by the President on October 25, 2005, Executive Order 13388 was crafted to strengthen the sharing and dissemination of terrorism information across government agencies. E.O. 13388 mandates that US departments and agencies give high priority to detecting, preventing, disrupting, preempting, and mitigating the effects of terrorist activities targeting the United States. Sharing information about these activities extends beyond the federal level to include state, local, and tribal governments, as well as appropriate private sector entities.

This Executive Order also establishes an Information Sharing Council chaired by the Program Manager and composed of designees of the Secretaries of State, the Treasury, Defense, Commerce, Energy, and Homeland Security; and the offices of the Attorney General; the DNI; the Director of the CIA; the Director of OMB; the Director of the FBI; and the Director of NCTC. This Council provides advice and information about an Information Sharing Environment to facilitate the automated sharing of terrorism information among appropriate agencies.

National Crime Information Center

FBI's National Crime Information Center (NCIC) maintains the Violent Gangs and Terrorist Organization File (VGTOF), which is a database indexing criminal information and terrorist identities. VGTOF can be made available to police officers on mobile patrol, thereby providing information immediately to frontline law enforcement officials.

Transportation Security Measures

Transportation Security Administration

The Transportation Security Administration (TSA) was established in the wake of the 9/11 attacks to strengthen passenger and baggage security at US airports and ensure that terrorists cannot stage similar attacks. Originally part of the Department of Transportation, TSA became part of DHS and is responsible for aviation security screening. Since February 2002, many security enhancements have been implemented through TSA to ensure the safety of travelers. Examples include the installation of hardened cockpit doors on commercial airlines and the use of canine teams to screen suspect baggage and cargo.

Federal Air Marshal Service

The modern day Federal Air Marshal Service (FAMS), which is a component of TSA, was established in 2001. Since the 9/11 attacks, FAMS has increased the number of semi-cover air marshals who provide enhanced security on US air carriers for both domestic and international flights. The FAMS' mission is to detect, deter, and defeat hostile acts targeting US air carriers, airports, passengers, and crews.

Secure Flight

Section 4012 of the IRTPA requires the TSA to pre-screen passengers using the consolidated terrorist watchlist maintained by the Federal government. The TSA Secure Flight program will fulfill this requirement. Under this program, which focuses on domestic US travelers, airlines will provide a limited set of passenger information to TSA when a reservation is made to determine whether a passenger should undergo further screening before boarding a plane or be denied boarding.

Northern Command

The Department of Defense established US Northern Command (NORTHCOM) in 2002 to consolidate under a single unified command existing missions that were executed previously by other military organizations. NORTHCOM is charged with Homeland defense and civil support, including conducting operations to deter, prevent, and defeat threats and aggression aimed at the United States, its territories, and interests within the assigned area of responsibility, and providing defense support of civil authorities as directed by the President or Secretary of Defense. NORTHCOM's Homeland defense mission is directed against military threats emanating from beyond US borders; however, the command has a cooperative relationship with federal agencies working to prevent terrorism. Information sharing and coordination enhance Homeland security efforts and may result in the prevention of threats, attacks, and other acts of aggression against the United States.

Strategic Objective 3: Strengthen US Identity Verification Systems

Significance

Official travel documents are key enablers of terrorist travel. Terrorists may travel around the world, including to the United States, with the object of targeting American interests and facilities. The US Government therefore must be concerned about the quality of the documents provided to its citizens, legal permanent residents, and non-immigrant visitors, as well as the documents of other countries used for travel to the United States. In protecting its Homeland, the US Government must consider the full range of documents—domestic as well as foreign—necessary to enter and remain in the United States. The ability to detect fraudulent travel documentation is vital to detecting terrorists as they travel.

Critical Mission Areas

- Standard Format and Security Features for Identification Documents and Improved Reporting of Lost or Stolen Passports
- Document Fraud Detection Initiatives
    - Detect and reduce travel document fraud in the domestic travel system
    - Continue to train federal, state, and local officials to recognize counterfeit and altered documents

Current Initiatives

Standard Format and Security Features for Identification Documents

US Passport Enhancements

The US passport, recognized as one of the world's most secure and tamper-resistant identification credentials, is ICAO-compliant, state-of the-art, and machine-readable with a digitized photo. The Department of State's 10-year passport replacement program will ensure that passports issued or renewed after 2006 will employ features to ensure the ability to verify the identity of the passport holder and legitimacy of its issuance. The United States will begin issuing e-passports in the spring of 2006 and will be issuing only e-passports after October 26, 2006.

Document Standardization

A number of measures are underway to support standardization and additional security features of travel documents:

Illegal Immigration Reform and Immigration Responsibility Act (IIRAIRA). In 1996, the IIRAIRA mandated the creation of a uniform national format, content, and set of security features for US birth certificates, the most common document used to establish US citizenship. IIRAIRA also directed the Executive Branch to coordinate federal agencies and state statistic offices to develop standards for birth certificates, and authorized the Department of Health and Human Services to provide assistance for states to conform.

REAL ID Act. Signed into law in 2005, the REAL ID Act contains a number of provisions related to immigration reform and document security. Title II of the REAL ID Act calls for improved security for drivers licenses and personal identification cards, and establishes minimum document requirements and issuance standards for federal recognition. These requirements include mandatory facial image capture, physical security and personnel security for locations and persons involved in the production of licenses, and fraudulent document recognition training for employees engaged in the issuance of drivers licenses.

Western Hemisphere Travel Initiative (WHTI). As noted previously, the WHTI will require all US citizens, citizens of British Overseas Territory of Bermuda, and citizens of Canada and Mexico to present a passport or other accepted secure document that establishes the bearer's identity and nationality to enter or re-enter the United States. WHTI will be implemented in phases between now and January 1, 2008. In response to this initiative, DHS has proposed acceptance of a card in lieu of a passport. Additionally, the Departments of State and Homeland Security have begun developing a lower-cost alternative to a traditional passport for use in crossing land borders. The system will be known as PASS (People Access Security System).

Database of US Lost and Stolen Passports

Since 2003, the United States has established and maintained an electronic database to record reported lost and stolen US passports. US regulations have also been changed to specify that, once reported to this database, the passport is no longer valid for travel. Information in this database is used at the border to screen for travelers using a passport that has been reported lost or stolen. Multiple losses are subject to investigation.

Document Fraud Detection Initiatives

Immigration and Customs Enforcement Forensic Document Laboratory

The ICE Forensic Document Laboratory (FDL) focuses on detecting fraudulently obtained genuine travel documents by bribing corrupt officials or submitting false information, and on assisting government officers to identify fraud. This is done in many ways, including providing expert forensic examination of questioned documents and developing specialized training programs on fraud detection that are used across the Federal government. The FDL staff of certified government experts provides training on document examination and document fraud to federal, state, and local officials, as well as to foreign government officials as part of ongoing US Government initiatives.

Pillar II: Continuing Challenges and Proposed Actions

As the current initiatives demonstrate, the United States has undertaken a number of steps since 9/11 to prevent terrorists from entering, traveling within, and operating successfully in the United States. This section lists five categories of continuing challenges, followed by corresponding proposed actions necessary to achieve continued success in denying terrorists the ability to enter, exit, and travel within the United States:

- Terrorist Screening and Information Sharing

- US Border Security

- US Document Security

- Immigration Laws and Policies

- Intelligence Capabilities and Training

The proposed actions are to be conducted within the constraints of US laws, especially those aimed at protecting the privacy and civil liberties of US persons.

Terrorist Screening and Information Sharing

Identifying potential terrorists is the first step in preventing them from entering and traveling within the United States. Building on current efforts, the US Government should:

(13) Consistent with Homeland Security Presidential Directive 11, finalize transition of the US Visitor and Immigrant Status Indicator Technology (US-VISIT) system, including VWP travelers, and consular processing of visa applicants from a two-fingerprint to a ten-fingerprint screening system managed within established databases.

(14) Grant the appropriate security clearances to consular, CBP, and USCIS officers, and establish the required technical infrastructure to support the sharing of classified information on travelers with potential ties to terrorism.

(15) Leverage the Information Sharing Environment to establish minimum system interoperability standards for agencies involved in sharing information on terrorists' identities, and to establish systems' connectivity to state and local law enforcement agencies.

US Border Security

Since 9/11, the US Government has focused significant attention and resources on securing US borders. Building on these efforts, the US Government should:

(16) Fully implement the US-VISIT system across the immigration and border management enterprise.

(17) Implement pre-departure Advance Passenger Information System (APIS) to improve the US Government's ability to vet international air and sea passengers against the consolidated terrorist watchlist maintained by the Federal government to identify and interdict potential terrorists before they depart the United States.

(18) Establish international registered traveler programs, on a multilateral basis, with partner nations to increase advance information on a greater number of travelers and allow for increased scrutiny of higher risk travelers attempting entry into the United States.

(19) Fully implement US Government supporting plans for the National Strategy for Maritime Security to defend US coastlines from terrorists seeking entry into the United States by sea.

US Document Security

Official travel documents are key enablers of terrorist travel. As such, the US Government must ensure that domestic documents that facilitate travel are standardized and secure.

(20) Fully implement and leverage authorities of the REAL ID Act, and develop regulations for state motor vehicle bureaus and state bureaus of vital statistics.

Immigration Laws and Policies

The US Government maintains broad legal authority in the border environment to search conveyances, individuals, and personal effects, and to deny entry to non-US citizens who pose a potential terrorism threat. Still, current immigration laws and related policies should be enhanced to counter the continuing terrorist threat. To this end, the US Government should:

(21) Expand efforts to control borders, address interior enforcement and attack immigration fraud, including through the Secure Border Initiative (SBI).

Intelligence Capabilities and Training

Aside from increasing the quantity and quality of analysts and analysis, the ability to understand fundamental components of terrorist-related travel and document fraud is basic to any intelligence-driven effort against terrorist mobility. To enhance its existing capabilities in these areas, the US Government should:

(22) Ensure that an appropriate number of intelligence analysts in the US Intelligence Community are dedicated to the problem of global terrorist mobility.

(23) Increase the number of actionable leads to Immigration and Customs Enforcement (ICE) and FBI by continuing to develop analytical capabilities surrounding information derived from US-VISIT and other border security systems.

(24) Provide sufficient resources to enable the Human Smuggling and Trafficking Center (HSTC) to fulfill its responsibilities to conduct analysis of clandestine terrorist travel and support the US Government's coordination of efforts to combat terrorist travel, as required in Section 7202 of the IRTPA.

(25) Capitalize on curricula currently employed by CBP, the Federal Law Enforcement Training Center, ICE, and the US Secret Service to develop a comprehensive document fraud prevention curriculum to train federal, state, and local document issuers and reviewers on establishing document fraud prevention and risk management programs, intelligence methods used to identify fraudulent travel documents, and how intelligence analysts can support field operators whose work involves the review of travel documents.

Moving Forward

The significant efforts of the US Government to leverage the full range of instruments of national power at its disposal to combat terrorist travel worldwide are making the American people safer. US Government initiatives aimed at constraining terrorist mobility are severely limiting the ability of our terrorist enemies to plan and execute attacks against Americans and our allies. At home the US Government is working with state and local governments and law enforcement agencies to prevent terrorists from entering the country and perpetrating attacks within the United States. Overseas we are working closely with partner nations to diminish terrorists' capacity to cross international borders and to secure travel documents and funding.

We seek to deny safe harbor to terrorists wherever they are or seek to move. This strategy demonstrates the resolve of the US Government to strengthen international and US travel systems and make them as inhospitable as possible to our terrorist enemies. Building on the progress we have made in the years since 9/11, we will see continuing successes in constraining terrorist movements and in fortifying the will of the international community to devote increased attention and resources to this critical front in the War on Terror.

Last year the President stated that the terrorists "are as brutal an enemy as we have ever faced. They're unconstrained by any notion of our common humanity, or by the rules of warfare. No one should underestimate the difficulties ahead, nor should they overlook the advantages we bring to this fight." Indeed, we face continuing challenges in the overall War on Terror and in the fight against terrorist travel. Let it be known that the United States is confronting these challenges head on—and that the terrorists will inevitably lose the fight.

Appendix: List of Acronyms and Abbreviations

APEC	Asia-Pacific Economic Coordination
APIS	Advance Passenger Information System
ATA	Antiterrorism Assistance Program
CBP	Customs and Border Protection
CCD	Consolidated Consular Database
CIA	Central Intelligence Agency
CR	Counterterrorism Response
CTAG	Counterterrorism Action Group
CTC	Counterterrorism Committee
DHS	Department of Homeland Security
DNI	Director of National Intelligence
DOD	Department of Defense
DOE	Department of Energy
DOJ	Department of Justice
DOT	Department of Transportation
FAMS	Federal Air Marshal Service
FBI	Federal Bureau of Investigation
FDAU	Fraudulent Document Analysis Unit
FDL	Forensic Document Laboratory
FTTTF	Foreign Terrorist Tracking Task Force
HSPD	Homeland Security Presidential Directive
HSTC	Human Smuggling and Trafficking Center

ICAO	International Civil Aviation Organization
ICE	Immigration and Customs Enforcement
IIRAIRA	Illegal Immigration Reform and Immigration Responsibility Act
IMET	International Military Education and Training
INTERPOL	International Criminal Police Organization
IRTPA	Intelligence Reform and Terrorism Prevention Act of 2004
ISE	Information Sharing Environment
ISPS	International Ship and Port Facility Security
JITF-CT	Joint Intelligence Task Force—Combating Terrorism
JTTF	Joint Terrorism Task Force
LESC	Law Enforcement Support Center
NCTC	National Counterterrorism Center
NOA	Notice of Arrival
NORAD	North American Aerospace Defense Command
NSEERS	National Security Entry-Exit Registration System
NSMS	National Strategy for Maritime Security
NTC	National Targeting Center
NVMC	National Vessel Movement Center
ODNI	Office of the Director of National Intelligence
OSCE	Organization for Security and Cooperation in Europe
PASS	People Access Security System
SAFTI	Secure and Facilitated International Travel Initiative
SAO	Security Advisory Opinion

SBI	Secure Border Initiative
SEVIS	Student and Exchange Visitor Information System
SPP	Security & Prosperity Partnership
State	Department of State
TAS	Threat Analysis Section
TIP	Terrorist Interdiction Program
Treasury	Department of the Treasury
TSA	Transportation Security Administration
TSC	Terrorist Screening Center
TSWG	Technical Support Working Group
TTIC	Terrorist Threat Integration Center
USCG	US Coast Guard
USCIS	US Citizenship and Immigration Services
US-VISIT	United States Visitor and Immigrant Status Indicator Technology
VGTOF	Violent Gang and Terrorist Organization File
VSO	Visa Security Officer
VWP	Visa Waiver Program
WHTI	Western Hemisphere Travel Initiative